Greyhound

Canine Blur!

by Natalie Lunis

Consultant: Lee Livingood
Certified Dog Behavior Consultant
International Association of Animal Behavior Consultants
Author of *Retired Racing Greyhounds for Dummies*
Winner of the Dog Writers Association of America Award

BEARPORT
PUBLISHING

NEW YORK, NEW YORK

Credits

Cover and TOC, © Uli Schlotterbeck/Panther Media/age fotostock; 4–5, © Adriano Bacchella/NaturePL/SuperStock; 7, © Erich Lessing/Art Resource, NY; 8–9, © Christopher Furlong/Getty Images; 9BL, © Mark Raycroft/Minden Pictures; 9BC, © Richard Kolar/Animals Animals Enterprises; 9BR, © ndxphotos/Newscom; 10L, © Neil Setchfield/Alamy; 10R, © Dennis MacDonald/Alamy; 11, © Brian Cleary/bcpix/Photographers Direct; 12T, © Dennis MacDonald/Alamy; 12B, © Dennis MacDonald/Alamy; 13, © EcoPrint/Shutterstock; 14T, © Sam Clark/farlap-photography/Photographers Direct; 14B, © Gerard Lacz/Peter Arnold Inc.; 15T, © Andy Rouse/The Image Bank/Getty Images; 15B, © Andy Rouse/Stone/Getty Images; 16, © Judy Zatonski/Animal-Photography; 17, © Dennis MacDonald/age Fotostock/Superstock; 18, © Sally-Anne Thompson/Animal-Photography; 19, © Myrleen Pearson/Photographers Direct; 20, © Andrea Redecker/Cockatoo Dreaming Gallery; 21, © Carolyn McKeone/Photo Researchers Inc.; 22, © Jerry Shulman/SuperStock; 23TL, © Laila Kazakevica/Shutterstock; 23TC, © Waldemar Dabrowski/Shutterstock; 23TR, © Hedser van Brug/Shutterstock; 23BL, © Utekhina Anna/Shutterstock; 23BR, © Himagine/iStockphoto.

Publisher: Kenn Goin
Editorial Director: Adam Siegel
Creative Director: Spencer Brinker
Original Design: Debrah Kaiser
Photo Researcher: Omni-Photo Communications, Inc.

Library of Congress Cataloging-in-Publication Data

Lunis, Natalie.
  Greyhound : canine blur! / by Natalie Lunis.
      p. cm. — (Blink of an eye: superfast animals)
  Includes bibliographical references and index.
  ISBN-13: 978-1-936087-90-7 (library binding)
  ISBN-10: 1-936087-90-1 (library binding)
  1. Greyhounds—Juvenile literature. 2. Animal locomotion—Juvenile literature. I. Title.
  SF429.G8L86 2011
  636.753'4—dc22
                            2010010576

For more information, write to Bearport Publishing Company, Inc., 101 Fifth Avenue, Suite 6R, New York, New York 10003. Printed in the United States of America in North Mankato, Minnesota.

062010
042110CGA

10 9 8 7 6 5 4 3 2 1

Contents

The World's Fastest

The greyhound is the fastest dog in the world.

It can run at a speed of up to 40 miles per hour (64 kph).

The world's fastest human can run at a top speed of 23 miles per hour (37 kph). A pet cat can reach a top speed of 30 miles per hour (48 kph). A greyhound can run faster than both.

Human
23 mph / 37 kph

Cat
30 mph/48 kph

Greyhound
40 mph/64 kph

Hunting and Chasing

Greyhounds have been running fast for a long time.

They are one of the oldest **breeds**, or kinds, of dogs in the world.

Hundreds of years ago in Europe, they were raised as hunting dogs.

The tall, fast-running **canines** were especially useful for chasing and catching deer and rabbits.

In fact, they were so good at hunting that for a long time only kings were allowed to own them.

The Beginnings of the Breed

Arctic Ocean

NORTH AMERICA

England

EUROPE

ASIA

Atlantic Ocean

Pacific Ocean

AFRICA

Pacific Ocean

SOUTH AMERICA

Indian Ocean

AUSTRALIA

Southern Ocean

ANTARCTICA

N W E S

■ Where records about greyhounds were first kept

Greyhounds were raised as hunting dogs in many parts of Europe, but they got their start as an official breed in England during the 1800s. That's when people started keeping records about greyhounds and their puppies.

This painting of greyhounds hunting deer is more than 500 years old.

Running and Racing

Greyhounds and several other breeds of hunting dogs are known as **sight hounds**.

That means that they follow the animals they hunt mostly by sight—not by smell, the way many other hunting dogs do.

It also means that they are easy to train for racing.

Sight hounds are eager to chase anything that moves.

Some other breeds of sight hounds are whippets, salukis, and Afghan hounds. All these dogs are fast runners—but not as fast as greyhounds.

whippet

saluki

Afghan hound

Follow That Rabbit!

People who hunted with greyhounds also raced the dogs against one another.

They let a rabbit go ahead of the dogs to see which dog could follow the fastest.

Then, in the early 1900s, a new invention changed greyhound racing and made it into a much more popular sport.

The invention was a mechanical rabbit— a model of the animal that was driven by a motor.

The "rabbit" moved quickly around a racetrack while the greyhounds chased it.

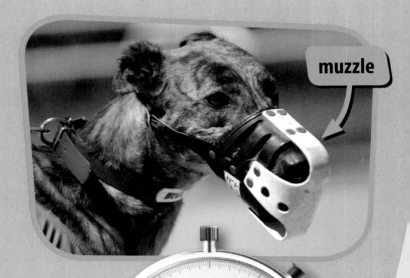

muzzle

During a race, greyhounds wear muzzles. These coverings help keep the dogs from biting other dogs that bump into them while running.

mechanical rabbit

mechanical rabbit

Flying Along

Greyhound races are short and fast.

After just three **strides**, the dogs can reach a speed of 40 miles per hour (64 kph).

The dogs seem to be flying as they gallop along.

In fact, all four of their feet leave the ground twice during each complete set of movements that the dogs make as they gallop.

A greyhound race is run over a distance of less than half a mile (.8 km) and usually lasts only about 30 seconds.

A Runner's Body

Many parts of a greyhound's body help it run fast.

Its long, bendable back allows its whole body to curl in and then spring out.

Because of this movement, each stride carries the greyhound forward more than the length of its body.

The greyhound's large heart and lungs carry the extra-large supply of blood and oxygen that its muscles need.

Its long tail helps it keep its balance during fast turns.

back curled in

springing forward

The way a greyhound's back curls and uncurls is similar to the way another animal's back moves while running. That animal is the cheetah. Racing along at up to 70 miles per hour (113 kph), it is the fastest runner in the world.

Needed: A New Home

Every year, thousands of racing greyhounds need new homes.

Why?

In some cases, they are injured or become too old to race.

In other cases, racetracks close, leaving the greyhounds without a place to live and work.

Luckily, however, groups in different parts of the United States are working to find new homes for the dogs.

retired greyhound racers

Most greyhounds
race for only two years.
They start when they are about
2 years old and stop when they
are about 4 years old. After
they stop racing, greyhounds
usually live for about
ten more years.

Excellent Pets

In the past, people thought that racing greyhounds wouldn't make good pets.

They thought that the canine athletes would be nervous and need lots of time and room to run.

Today, however, people are finding out that the dogs are in fact smart, loving, and easygoing pets.

Even though greyhounds can run faster than any other dog, they mostly love to relax at home with their owners.

Greyhounds enjoy being with other dogs.

Norfolk terriers

Staying in Shape

No matter how much they like to relax, pet greyhounds do need exercise.

To get it, they can run and play outside—though only in fenced-in areas.

A greyhound that gets loose might take off after a squirrel or other small animal—and be very hard to catch.

The dogs can also get the exercise they need if their owners put a leash on them and take them outside.

A run or walk is a great way to spend time together—and greyhounds will have no trouble keeping up!

An adult greyhound is 25 to 30 inches (64 to 76 cm) tall at the shoulder. It usually weighs from 55 to 80 pounds (25 to 36 kg).

Built for Speed

What makes a greyhound such a fast runner? Here is how different parts of the dog's body help it reach its amazing speeds.

long, flexible back makes it possible for the body to curl and uncurl—leading to long strides

pointy, narrow head cuts down on wind resistance, which is oncoming wind that can slow the animal's speed

long tail helps the dog keep its balance during fast turns

large heart and lungs send plenty of oxygen to muscles

long legs with strong muscles help with long, quick strides

long, narrow paws are good for pushing off the ground while running

Glossary

breeds (BREEDZ)
kinds of dogs

canines (KAY-nyenz)
members of the dog family

muzzles (MUH-zuhlz)
coverings put on dogs'
snouts, usually to keep
them from biting

sight hounds (SITE HOUNDZ)
dogs that hunt using mostly
their sense of sight, or seeing

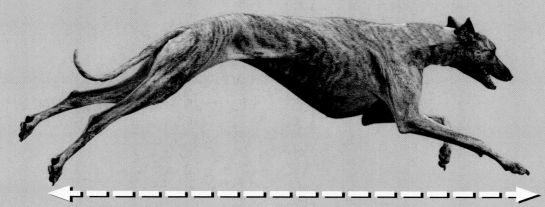

strides (STRYEDZ)
the distances covered in
steps taken by animals

Index

Read More

Meister, Cari. *Greyhounds*. Edina, MN: ABDO (2001).

Stout, Frankie. *Nature's Fastest Animals*. New York: PowerKids Press (2008).

Wilcox, Charlotte. *The Greyhound*. Mankato, MN: Capstone (2001).

Learn More Online

To learn more about greyhounds, visit
www.bearportpublishing.com/BlinkofanEye

About the Author

Natalie Lunis has written many science and nature books for children. She lives in the Hudson River Valley, just north of New York City.